Make friends with the Angels

SISTER EMMANUEL

Make friends

with

the Angels

children
of
Medjugorje

Edited by Ann-Marie Chinnery, Rosalia Schlett, Fr David Chinnery, Fr Gabriele M. White, OJSS.
Cover design by Nancy Cleland.
Book design by Catholic Way Publishing.

Ordering Information:
Orders by trade bookstores and wholesalers.
Please contact Ingram Content at www.ingramcontent.com.

ISBN-13: 978-1-7377881-9-5 (Paperback)

10 9 8 7 6 5 4 3 2 1

Available in E-Book.

Children of Medjugorje
www.childrenofmedjugorje.com

Contents

ANGELS ARE REAL!

In the world you have the visible universe: you have the trees, the sky, the fields, the fruit, the houses... you have the earth. You have everything you can touch, see, and hear; but you also have the invisible universe and the invisible universe is actually much wider, much richer, and much more immense than the visible universe. The Angels are part of the invisible universe but there is a difference between something that is 'invisible' and something that is 'unreal.' You can be invisible and still be very real... more real than the trees and the earth and the grass in your garden! The Angels are part of this invisible world but they are absolutely real, and to ignore them is a big mistake. So, let's try to discover together who they are, what they do, why they are by our side, why they are supposed to lead us, what is their role/mission, how they have been created and what their characteristics are.

To start with, I would like to tell you a story so that you can start to connect with them in a very practical and real way. It is a story of what happened to some very good friends of mine in Medjugorje. This little group of people were actually on vacation in Munich, Germany, and they had to go back to Medjugorje by car. One of them, however, felt a very strong urge to go and see a priest in Italy called Father Luigi Bosio, (now a Venerable and in the process of Beatification) who lived in a little apartment adjoined to the Cathedral of Verona.

Now from a practical point of view that was a bizarre thing to do because this detour would add five long hours to the drive, and besides this, the priest was very ill and was confined to bed. He had stopped receiving visitors for some months.

Leading up to his apartment there was a private gate and then a second door which was usually locked. Since they were travelling on a Sunday, they knew that on Sundays there would be no one there to open the door. So, there were three obstacles to be crossed. But because this priest was exceptional—not only holy but exceptional—and very gifted, they wanted to try and see him because just meeting his gaze exuded God in the most extraordinary way. Their desire for a blessing from him was very strong... stronger than the obstacles in their way, so they decided to go for it.

While on the road they decided to try to call him. The call went through to his answering machine and the message left on the machine said that Fr. Bosio does not receive visitors but he will answer the phone between 4 and 5pm. This small gap was impossible for them considering their tight travel schedule. So again, from a human standpoint their plan was doomed to fail before it had even started.

Then, do you know what they did? This little group of friends decided to put their Guardian Angels to work. First, they requested that the Angels go to Fr. Bosio and ask him if they could come, and then return with his answer back to them. After praying for a few minutes and trying to hear the answer of the Angels, a great joy filled their hearts, and so this encouraged them to continue driving towards Verona. Every half an hour they would pray to their Guardian Angels and send them again to Fr. Bosio to make sure he was warned that they were coming and to make sure they could get in.

So, when they arrived in Verona next to the Cathedral, the first gate was wide open! Extraordinary... so they went in, parked the car and they found that the entrance door of the apartment building was also wide open! They started walking up the stairs which leads to Fr. Bosio's floor and guess who they saw... Fr. Bosio himself! He was standing on the last step of the staircase waiting for them! They heard his voice saying, "Ah here you are, you who have sent me your Guardian Angels every half hour. Come in! I want to give you a blessing."

What a wonderful welcome they received!

Our Guardian Angels are
a great gift from God

Now in Medjugorje the visionaries tell us that when Our Lady appears, especially on great feast days like Easter, Christmas, All Saints Day, the Assumption and so on, she comes with a few Angels and sometimes she is surrounded with many Angels. When she appears on Mount Krizevac (Cross Mountain) some of the visionaries tell me that the mountains are covered with Angels. It is incredible! Mary, of course, is the Queen of Angels and when she travels, she does so with her friends–like we all do.

People have asked the visionaries "What do the Angels look like?" They tell us that they look like little children and that they have wings. They look at their Queen, and this is very important—they are fascinated by her; they admire her so much and everything she does they mimic. If she is very happy and she is delivering a very happy message they will show their happiness by moving their wings and on their face, you see them smiling. The longer the apparition lasts the happier they become. Sometimes they get so excited and they become so happy, that their wings become very noisy when they move them—it's very funny.

But on the contrary when Our Lady is sad, and you know she often has many reasons to be sad, then they are very distraught. They express their sadness, it's very touching. They mimic everything she does and they are very attached to her.

Of course, the reality of the Angels is not new, it's not something we have learned through Medjugorje. They are mentioned throughout the Bible and throughout the history of the people of God. In the story of creation, when we read the book of Genesis the Angels are already there in the Garden of Eden and of course God is the Creator of the Angels. We see in the scriptures how the Angels serve God. For example, in the Old Testament God sends the Angels to execute his orders, to provide things for his people, he uses them to give messages to his prophets, to lead the people. There are many apparitions of the Angels throughout the Bible.

One of my favourite passages is in the book of Exodus in the Bible when God gave to Moses, the leader of his people, a special Angel just for him. He says to him "See, I am sending an Angel ahead of you to guard you along the way and to bring you to the place I have prepared. Pay attention to him and listen to what he says. Do not rebel against him; he will not forgive your rebellion, since my Name is in him. If you listen carefully to what he says and do all that I say, I will be an enemy to your enemies and will oppose those who oppose you. My Angel will go ahead of you and bring you into the land of the Amorites, Hittites, Perizzites, Canaanites, Hivites and Jebusites, and I will wipe them out." (Ex. 23:20-23)

Right at the beginning of Jesus' life we see the Angel Gabriel announcing to Mary that she has been chosen to conceive Baby Jesus in her womb. Then later we see another Angel in Bethlehem telling the Good News to the shepherds in the field at night and then an army of Angels joining him with praise to God—Gloria in excelsis Deo! That's what they were singing.

When Jesus went into the desert, after His baptism, when He spent 40 days there fasting and praying, we again see the Angel coming to Him and serving Him (Mt. 4:11). When Jesus speaks about the little children, He says "do not rebuke the little children, for I tell you: their Angels in heaven continually see the face of my Father in heaven" (Mt. 18:10). Each of our Guardian Angels too contemplates the face of God. This passage in the Bible helps us to realize and believe that we all have a Guardian Angel and we should be happy about it because it is a great gift! Yes, we all have a special Angel for each one of us alone and whether we want one or not it is there. Too many people today do not care about that or they do not know about this reality. Actually, it's not an option, it is Church doctrine, it is part of our faith. Catholics believe in the existence of Angels and we believe that we have been given a Guardian Angel.

I want here to highlight paragraph 328 from the Catechism of the Catholic Church—a book that we should all have at home and read regularly—where it talks about the Guardian Angels "The existence of the spiritual, non-corporeal beings that Sacred Scripture usually calls 'Angels' is a truth of faith. The witness of Scripture is as clear as the unanimity of Tradition."

So, as I mentioned, it is not an option to believe in the Angels—it's right there in the Catechism, and we have to believe it.

I will share with you something that happened to a priest friend of mine in Paris, many years ago. When he was just a seminarian, he had the great opportunity to go to Confession to Padre Pio in San Giovanni Rotondo, Italy. Now during confession Padre Pio asked him, "Do you sometimes pray to your Guardian Angel?" My friend answered, "No, you must be kidding, I don't believe in Guardian Angels." Then do you know what happened?—Padre Pio slapped him in the face, and said to him, "Silly! Stupid! I see him by your side!" I think it slapped some sense into him because my friend from that day forward started to pray to his Guardian Angel! It was a blessed slap! Praise God.

Another passage in the Catechism of the Catholic Church about the Guardian Angels is at paragraph 336: "From its beginning until death, human life is surrounded by their watchful care and intercession. Beside each believer stands an Angel as protector and shepherd leading him to life. Already here on earth the Christian life shares by faith in the blessed company of Angels and men united in God."

So, we believe as Catholics that at the very moment of our conception we all have a special Angel appointed to us by God so that we might be led by him in our life.

Don't ignore the Angels!

I want to share with you my own personal testimony of my experience with my Guardian Angel. When I was a young child, my parents told me about Guardian Angels, so from childhood I was familiar with my Guardian Angel and I even gave him a name—I called him Raphael. This made it easier for me to call upon him. It was also the name of an Archangel and so I thought it was a good name. I treated him like my companion—I would send him to do various tasks, and to various people, and ask for his help in different situations, and I must say he has always been very efficient and helpful. He has protected me so much—I don't think I would still be alive today without him.

When I entered the Community of the Beatitudes in France, I found myself in our little convent in Nazareth. We were only four sisters in the house, and two brothers were not far away in another house. Of course, I would share with the sisters my stories about my Guardian Angel. One of the sisters was called Sylvie, and she was from a Protestant background. Although she was now a Catholic, she would not pray to the Angels because she was sceptical about that. Still, she would listen to my stories.

She was quiet and she would listen to our prayer to the Angels and inside she would think, "What is this? How can they pray to their Guardian Angels like this?" She thought it was weird. However, I would continue to share about my adventures with my Guardian Angel and how helpful he was—all the stories that happened to me with him. Even though she thought it was strange, she found the idea quite attractive and thought, "what if this is real?"

So, one day she wanted to test whether the Angels are real. There was something she wanted to tell me that I had done wrong, but she was too timid to say it to me. Since she knew that I called my Guardian Angel, Raphael, she simply said to him "Raphael if you are really as great as Sr. Emmanuel says, if you can really do jobs and if you can really help us, then I want to know. So please today tell sister this particular thing (she mentioned what he had to tell me) because I don't have the confidence to tell her myself so it's your job to tell her and if you tell her and I have the proof that you've spoken to her then I will believe that we can pray to the Angels. Otherwise forget it." That was her prayer.

She made that prayer in the morning. Of course, I did not know that she had made this test, and off I went to my work. At that time, I was working in the Italian hospital in Nazareth. I would work half a day and then return for lunch. I will never forget this; I opened the door and the three other sisters were at the table and had already started eating their lunch. Before I even greeted them, I said "guess what the Lord has told me today in prayer," and believe me I repeated exactly word for word the message that Sylvie had given to my Guardian Angel. Her jaw dropped to the table, dumbfounded. At that moment she said nothing to me because she had to reflect on it but she was completely overwhelmed. Then, a while later, she told me the whole story and that's how I found out and she said, "You know sister, from that day on I started praying to my Guardian Angel and to your Guardian Angel and to all the Angels." She became one of the best employers of Guardian Angels I ever met in my entire life.

Well now, some people would say "No I don't pray to my Guardian Angel because I only want to pray to Jesus, only Jesus is God. I'm not going to pray to creatures. I don't want anything to get in the way. I deal directly with Jesus." It is very good to deal directly with Jesus, I don't say otherwise—it's good. But what if you exclude those that He, Jesus himself, has given you as friends? Do you think you please Him this way? No, you just offend Him and you sadden him.

Now suppose you have a beautiful fiancé and you love your fiancé and this fiancé of course has a mom, a dad, she has brothers and sisters and she has friends too. One day you go to her home to see your fiancé but the mom opens the door, and you don't care because she is only the mom, she's not the fiancé. Then the brothers show up and you don't care because it is just her brothers. If you say, "where is my fiancé I only want to speak with her, I don't care about you guys I want only her," don't you think that she will be very sad about this?

Surely, she will say to you, "let me introduce you to my mom, she is part of my life and she knows me so well. So as a fiancé if you want to see me, to know me and to know who I really am, go to her and she will tell you stories about my childhood. You will know me better and hopefully you will love me more. Also, this is my brother, let me introduce you to him, he had a great influence on me, and this is my sister and this is my family and this is my dad and I love each of the members of my family. So, if you want to really love me then share that love with my family. Then they will become part of your family as we are one family now."

You cannot just cut them off. Jesus Himself gave a Guardian Angel to each one of us so if you want to please Jesus, you will please Him a lot by praying to the Angels. The Angels belong to Jesus, He is the king of Angels so of course Jesus is very happy when we pray to them.

I want to remind you of some of the passages in the Bible that talk about the Angels and it shows how Jesus is not only the king of the Angels but the Creator of the Angels. These passages explain how the Angels relate to Him, how they belong to Him. Christ is the centre of the Angelic world; they are his Angels. In the Gospel of Matthew, it says "When the Son of Man comes in his glory, and all the holy Angels with him, then he will sit on the throne of his glory. Before him all the nations will be gathered, and he will separate them one from another." (Mt. 25:31-32) You see, Jesus will come with His Angels who are His companions on the last day when He returns to Earth. He will be surrounded by thousands of Angels. That is from the Gospel.

We know that the Angels have been created by Him and for Him and through Him, "For in him all things were created: things in heaven and on earth, visible and invisible, whether thrones or powers or rulers or authorities; all things have been created through Him and for Him" (Col. 1:16). Now they belong to Him even more since He has made them messengers of His plan of salvation. We see that the Angels have been present throughout creation and throughout the history of man and they will be eternally present with us. Their mission and their job is to help us. The more we pray to them the more they manifest their help to us. That is very clear, you will see for yourself.

Let me tell you another story. I remember one time I was in Jerusalem with my community and there were six of us. We were invited to give our testimonies in a convent run by Poor Clares and the sisters had gathered some friends, benefactors, and family members for the conference. There were about 50 people. Unfortunately, when we arrived, they were all talking to each other very loudly and when we heard the noise, we could tell that it was going to be very difficult to share our testimonies with them because their hearts were not open to listen. You cannot be attentive to God in the noise.

We were quite sad about this, but my sister Sylvie, the same one I mentioned earlier, smiled at me and she said, "Listen, let us use our Guardian Angels. Let's put them to work and make a deal with them. Let's gather all of them and we will pray to all of them here present which means 50 Guardian Angels and we will ask them in prayer—please tell your protege to keep quiet".

Now you will not believe it but right away all the agitation in the room disappeared and a very deep incredible silence fell on the room. For no obvious reason, in a matter of seconds everybody stopped their conversation and a wonderful peace settled on us. It was phenomenal. So, thanks to the silence we prayed first to the Holy Spirit and we started to give witness and to speak about God, and the people really listened very carefully.

You see, it took the idea to use the Angels and it was an incredible experience. We were shocked at the efficiency and the power of the Guardian Angels—we were so grateful to them.

Another time I remember I was going to speak at a conference about Medjugorje and it was in a church where about 2000 people were expected. Now this took place in a country where I knew the people were quite serious and it was kind of heavy for me because when I speak, I like to make little jokes but I knew that it was likely that these people would not laugh at my jokes. I was a bit anxious and stressed. So I cast my mind back to my time in Nazareth and all these experiences with the Angels and I thought to myself, when Jesus was born in Bethlehem there were many Angels there who were exuding with joy at the birth of the Messiah and so I made this request to them: "Dear Angels of Bethlehem you know the situation I am in, therefore I beg you to place yourself at the side of each person and also to fill the entire church. Take away any heaviness there when I speak and bring joy in abundance so the atmosphere becomes light and highly spiritual and that Our Lady's message may go straight to the heart of every person."

When I finished my prayer, I started speaking and very quickly I noticed that all the faces in front of me started to light up with joy! It was so encouraging and I thought wow what good Angels! But then my surprise doubled when I noticed they started laughing when I had not even said anything funny. So 20 minutes into my talk the whole assembly was laughing so much that I had to kind of secretly send a little word to the troop of Angels and I said to them: "Well dear Angels of Bethlehem, okay you are doing a wonderful job you are spreading your great spirit of joy and I am very thankful, but listen, if they continue to laugh like this I won't be able to fit in my talk, so please can you just cool down a little bit so that I am able to finish". It was really incredible. That night the audience was so open and so joyful it was phenomenal. The atmosphere was very open and friendly, I was so happy. So once again the Angels had dazzled me with how quickly they answered my prayer.

Now remember if you are somewhere where the atmosphere is serious and heavy, appeal to the Angels of Bethlehem—their sense of humour will emanate to all those who are present. Don't leave the Angels idle; give them some jobs to do!

Where does the word 'Angel' come from? In Hebrew, the word for Angel is *malach*. The root of this word means 'to be sent.' When you send someone to give a message to someone who is far away, this man is called malach in Hebrew meaning messenger. So, by nature the Angels are messengers and this is why we can use them to send messages to others.

All the saints use Angels, they use them a lot. For example, Pope Pius XI, Pope John XXIII, St. Padre Pio, St. Faustina, you have many saints who used their Guardian Angels very often in a powerful way.

Let us think about St. Padre Pio for a moment—he was a very holy man, very powerful but also very famous. Because he was so famous, holy, and charismatic, he had many spiritual children all over the world and especially in Italy. Those spiritual children would write letters to him—there were no emails at that time—and they would tell him their problems, concerns, and sufferings. They would also tell him very deep things about their souls, but like all of us, St. Padre Pio only had 24 hours in the day, so how could he possibly answer all those letters? Impossible! He also spent hours and entire days in the confessional, so there was no way he could answer all those letters. So, what did he do? Actually, he had a very special relationship with his Guardian Angel. He would see him sometimes, and talk to him often as his companion and of course he would put him to work.

The more you ask from your Guardian Angel in prayer, the more powerful he answers you and manifests himself. So, Padre Pio, in the best way possible, would ask his Guardian Angels to answer these letters, and they just did it! Padre Pio would tell them, "You see this pile of letters—make sure they're answered."

The Guardian Angels were in charge of answering the letters. Since they are Angels, they can read thoughts and they know what is going on in people's lives. So, they knew exactly what Padre Pio would have said and they knew what the thoughts of Padre Pio would be to enable them to answer those people who were in need of grace. So, if ever you received a letter from Padre Pio during his life, well, I am sorry I'm not sure that he would have written it himself, it might have been his Guardian Angel—who knows?

WE HAVE MORE THAN ONE ANGEL

One thing we all must know is that when we were conceived, we all received a Guardian Angel for our life and they will be with us for all eternity. When we die, our Guardian Angel is never appointed to another person, they remain with us and cling to us for all eternity. He will be our eternal special friend (except for those who go to Hell).

Now do not be mistaken and think we have only one Angel. We have one Guardian Angel, but we have other Angels too. Actually, we may have several. I will give you an example, if I get married and I have a family, God will extend an Angel to keep my family and this Angel will be the Angel of the family. If I become a priest, the Lord will send an Angel especially for my priesthood to keep me and to help me to be a good and holy priest. If I become a bishop, I will have another Angel which is especially appointed for me being a bishop, to be a good bishop. If I am the Pope, there will be a special Angel appointed by God for the Pope. If I am a doctor there is a special Angel for doctors. If I am an artist/ painter/sculptor, there is a special Angel for artists. If I am a nurse there is a special Angel for me. In other words, whatever profession I have there is a special Angel for me. If I belong to a community there is a special Angel for the community. If I enter the Carmelite Convent, there is a special Angel for that Carmelite Convent.

Now, if I live in a city, for example Johannesburg, Paris, London, or New York there is a special Angel appointed by God for that city that I can pray to. Do you remember when the Angels appeared to the little shepherds in Fatima, (those who saw Our Lady)? The Angel told them, "I am the Angel of Portugal." He was the special Angel for Portugal, and we know that the Angel of Portugal was actually the Angel of the Eucharist. So, if I see terrible things happening in my city, for example satanism, suicides, crime, and bad leadership from the politicians, I have the Guardian Angel of that city to pray to and I can make friends with him and he will work at making the city a better place.

God has created human nature but also the Angelic nature. We have a human nature which means we have a spirit and a body. The Angelic nature is a pure Spirit that has no body. This means that they only have a spirit, but this gives them an incredible freedom because they are not limited by space and time. So why do we see them sometimes in pictures and paintings like little babies with wings, and why did the visionaries in Medjugorje see them in the same way? This is just a symbolic body—it is not their real body. But we need to be able to spot them—if it is a painting, we have to see them to help us realise what they do. Their wings are a symbol to show that they can act very fast because they are a pure spirit. They don't really have wings.

Now we know and we learn from St. Paul that man is superior to the Angels. Why? It is not because we are smarter— definitely not! Actually, Angels are much smarter than us. This is only because Jesus, the Son of God, took on the human nature so He gave to human nature the glory that the Angelic nature does not have. This is why we are above the Angels in the creation of God, but we should not forget that we ourselves are very weak. The body we have makes us blind and heavy. We can also become sick, tired, discouraged, exhausted and we also die. Now the heaviness of our body makes us live in a certain darkness, but the Angels live in the full light of God and are very smart, very intelligent.

An Angel as a spiritual being has the capacity to reach us within our being and to influence us. Of course, God alone has access to the deepest depth of our souls where we hold that wedding chamber, but around that, we have layers/chambers of ourselves and Angels have access to the outer ones. For example, they can access our thoughts, our will, our memories, our imagination, our sensitivity, and the Angels have access to our body too. We should be aware of that and make friends with our Angels who can help us so much. Let us keep that in mind, and for example if you are tired then pray to your Guardian Angel and if it is God's plan then he can unburden you from your tiredness. If you are in a scary situation pray to your Angels—they can be like bodyguards, but even better.

Angels are much more powerful than human beings and they are invincible. They are quicker and smarter and they know the plans of your enemies. Power is not just in muscles! So, Angels can also help us to do things. Here is an example, perhaps you know about the little Carmelite sister called Maryam of Bethlehem—she was born in the 19th century just before St Therese, the Little Flower, and she lived in Israel. Even though she was sick, one day she was asked to clean a huge room for a sister who needed the room and it needed to be available very quickly. This job felt impossible for her because she was so ill and there was not enough time to do it, but she agreed to do the job because she was very holy.

After a short while another sister entered the room and she saw that the whole job was done in no time at all. The sister was really surprised and she asked St Maryam of Bethlehem how she did it so quickly, and she responded simply, "The children helped me." This was how she spoke; she was very simple. She did not know how to read and write and she used to call Angels 'the children.' She was very familiar with the children/Angels. In fact, what had happened was the Angels cleaned the room for her because Angels can access our feelings.

The Angels also have access to our sexuality. Suppose someone has a sexual attraction to someone which does not fit with God's plan for humanity and for marriage, the Guardian Angels are very good at directing us along the right path.

I remember a very holy priest confided to me that when he was a young priest, he had an incredible attraction to a woman. She was very nice and she would go to him sometimes for confession. He was so tempted by her, and so whenever he would speak to her, he would make sure there was always a table between them because it was such a strong attraction. It was a real suffering for him, because as a priest he did not want to give into the temptation. He told me one day that he prayed three times a special prayer to Our Lady, the Queen of the Angels, and he said that in no time at all the spirit of lust he had was gone and he could look at that woman and there was no more attraction there. That's the Guardian Angels! It was a bad Angel that influenced his sexuality. You can see from this testimony how the Angels have access to our sexuality.

St. Michael the Archangel is particularly powerful. You can pray novenas to St. Michael and you will see the result for yourself as well as for others. Angels have access to our imagination and to our dreams. Remember St. Joseph had dreams sometimes and the Angels would speak to him through those dreams telling him important things that he needed to know to enable him to be a Good Shepherd for the holy family. It was an Angel who told Joseph not to be afraid to take Mary as his wife when she was pregnant. It was again an Angel who told him to flee to Egypt when they were under threat from King Herod. An Angel also told him when it was safe to return to his homeland from Egypt because King Herod had died. As you can see, Joseph did not need CNN or the BBC. Angels would deliver the news to him. There is no mixture with the truth with Angels, just plain light.

Angels know God's plan for us, they know about our vocation, they know what the dream of our Creator is for us and they see it very clearly. They are in charge to help us live it and realise it in its fullness and fulfil our vocation.

Now suppose the Lord wishes a little boy to become a priest. Of course, his Guardian Angel will know about it and he will do everything he can to help this little boy from his childhood to avoid everything that could harm or block his vocation. This Guardian Angel will lead him on his path, he will help him to stay pure and pray to God, worship God, listen to his word and do his will. He will help the little boy to be charitable, to think of others, to give himself in service for others, to be attentive and he will help him in any way so that this little boy may reach the goal of becoming a priest, and then a holy priest.

Now, this is a little personal family testimony. When my mom was young, she would always pray to her Guardian Angel and she would pray to him for the man who the Lord had in store for her as a husband. She would ask her Guardian Angel to protect him and to lead him and she would also pray to the Guardian Angel of that boy. Little did she know that my father, who was part of the French Resistance, would have to spend three years in the Nazi concentration camps in Germany. He was the only one from his section of ten men to return home alive.

My mother met him after the war and they got married. When my mom told my dad about those prayers that she was addressing to her Guardian Angel and his Guardian Angel, my dad was absolutely astounded because he had also done the same thing! He prayed to his Angel for the wife the Lord had prepared for him and he would pray to the Guardian Angel of his future wife that she would be kept for him. As a matter of fact, the first minute he saw my mom he knew that she was the one.

Now God has a plan for each one of our lives and the Angels are the keepers/guardians of that plan. Their job is to help us realize that plan in its fullness and they always lead us back to it when we go astray. So, when we are searching for our vocation, our Guardian Angel can help us greatly. Our Angels are counsellors too; we might not see them but they are definitely by our side to help us and lead us each day on the right path.

We can pray to the Angels to free us from the influences of demons because demons are Angels too. Just as the good Angels of God are meant to influence us for good out of love for us (they love us the way God loves us), the demons are constantly working to inject their poison into us with the very clear goal for us to be lost, body and soul. They are destroyers; and as Angels they have the same capacity to influence those parts of us that our Guardian Angels can: our imagination, feelings, and our will. These parts of us can be influenced by demons. Our will can be weakened by demons. They can confuse our minds and remove the little peace we have.

If we live in sin we are surrounded by demons because they have a way in through the sin. Every sin opens a new door to them depending on the seriousness of the sin. Even when we are not aware of the danger or the reality of sin, we remain vulnerable to evil. Take for example a little 3-year-old boy: he is playing in the house and he does not know that putting his finger in the electrical socket could kill him. It is not his fault, nobody told him. But because he doesn't know that it is wrong, he does it and what happens—there is a deadly shock that electrocutes him. He is not excluded from receiving the shock because he does not know the danger.

It is the same for us with sin. Take for example the sin of abortion. If a girl does not know that it is a serious sin, her moral culpability before God for that action is not as great, but the harm happens all the same. Ignorance has never been a virtue.

I need to say something very important about demons because they are also part of the invisible world. When God created the Angels, they were all good, there were no demons. God never created demons; the Angels were created by God in His light and they are creatures of light. But just like us, they had to go through a test and the test was a choice—they had to choose to be with God and serve Him and His plans or not, because being in heaven with God is not automatic. Nobody gets to Heaven without a free choice. We are free to say yes to God and because we are free to say yes, we are also free to say no. You cannot be free to say yes without being free to say no, otherwise what kind of freedom is that?

Think about it, if somebody tells you that he loves you but then you find out that this person had no other option but to love you, he had to love you, what kind of love is that? On the other hand, if you find out that this person had 100 opportunities not to love you and still, he chooses to be with you and to love you then that is real love.

Love and freedom go together, there is no love without freedom. So, God who loves us perfectly waits for us to choose freely to be with Him, and this is why there is that test. When God created the Angels, they were free to choose Him and to agree with His plans or not and some Angels unfortunately chose to oppose God. They refused to serve His plans. They disconnected themselves from God who is the source of good and they became evil spirits because there is no good and no light away from God. There is not a place where you can be good in the darkness which is away from God, it does not exist.

The evil spirits kept the characteristics of their nature but they use them for wrong purposes. The Catechism of the Catholic Church tells us "Scripture speaks of a sin of these Angels. This 'fall' consists in the free choice of these created spirits, who radically and irrevocably *rejected* God and his reign. We find a reflection of that rebellion in the tempter's words to our first parents: 'You will be like God.' The devil 'has sinned from the beginning;' he is 'a liar and the father of lies.'" (paragraph 392) Here you have the word 'irrevocably.' This means that the Angels do not have the ability to reform as we human beings do here on earth. They remain stuck in their final choice of saying 'no' to God.

Paragraph 393 of the Catechism says "It is the *irrevocable* character of their choice, and not a defect in the infinite divine mercy, that makes the Angels' sin unforgivable. There is no repentance for the Angels after their fall, just as there is no repentance for men after death."

Since they are Angels, they do not have the same blindness like we do, and so it was with full consciousness that they said 'no' to God. This is different to us humans who are so blind, we have no idea what it is to be in the full light of God. This is why we can always change our 'no' into a 'yes.' During our lifetime on earth, we can always reform ourselves and repent, but when we reach our last hour there comes a moment when we make our final choice for eternity. At the point of our earthly death, and before we reach our eternal destination, Jesus told Venerable Marthe Robin and St. Faustina that He gives the soul one last opportunity in the light of God to decide for heaven or not (§1486, St. Faustina's Diary).

So, either you choose God and humbly ask for forgiveness for your sins to receive His mercy and enter Heaven or purgatory if you need first to be purified. Or you can decide to reject God. If you say many little no's to God during your whole life you might also reject God at the last moment and with that choice you will be without Him for eternity. You send yourself directly to hell. If you say many little yeses to Him, you may say a big yes to Him when you see Him.

When Our Lady showed the visionaries of Medjugorje hell, they asked her, "How can this be?" She said, "These are people who choose to go there with all their freedom in the full light." (Our Lady to the prayer group in the early years of the apparitions) Once you are in heaven you do not go out, you do not even think to go out—that would be silly!

Even in purgatory the souls know they have received salvation and although they suffer a lot from their time of purification they would not like to go back to earth where there is so much darkness. However, if you are in hell, it means you do not want to receive anything from God and you stay there forever. It is not that God does not want you but rather you do not want God, you hate God; this is what the word 'irrevocable' means, a total rejection of God and His grace forever.

Let me share with you another passage from the Catechism because it explains very well the fall of the Angels, "Behind the disobedient choice of our first parents lurks a seductive voice, opposed to God, which makes them fall into death out of envy. Scripture and the Church's Tradition see in this being a fallen Angel, called "Satan" or the "devil". The Church teaches that Satan was at first a good Angel, made by God: "The devil and the other demons were indeed created naturally good by God, but they became evil by their own doing." (paragraph 391)

Lucifer, whose name means 'he who carries the light' was a very bright Angel, but when he was tested, he said no to God, he rebelled against the will of God and therefore he fell. Although he had the same character as the other Angels, he chose to use all his power against God and the creatures of God. This is why, by the way, he pursues us and his job, contrary to our Guardian Angels, is to separate us from God and to lead us astray from the will of God and God's plan for our life. We are surrounded by thousands of these bad Angels, the rebellious ones who are trying so hard to separate humanity from God.

In Medjugorje Our Lady said, "Satan is strong and desires to destroy not only human life but also nature and the planet on which you live. Therefore, dear children pray that through prayer you can protect yourself with God's blessing of peace." (January 25, 1991) She also said, "Dear children, Satan is strong and is waiting to test each one of you. Pray, and that way he will neither be able to injure you nor block you on the way of holiness." (September 25, 1987)

Now let me explain the word 'faith.' In Hebrew faith is 'emunah' and emunah means adhesion, when we adhere to God and are one with him. The devil is par excellence the disconnected one from God. So, when we have faith, we are connected to God and the devil cannot harm us. By permission of God, the demons know us and they know our weaknesses. They have the same intelligence as the other Angels, they are very smart, very cunning, and this is why it is very important not to address any demon. Do not speak to them, do not start a conversation with them.

Eve in the Garden of Eden spoke to the serpent directly and she fell into sin because she believed every word the serpent said to her even though the words opposed what God had said. Remember the serpent (Satan) is a liar and he is the father of lies, so do not speak to them even if you are tormented. Go to Jesus, go to Mary, go to your Guardian Angel, and ask them to protect you from the evil one but do not address Satan directly unless you are a priest or an exorcist. It is too dangerous; you will get trapped.

In Medjugorje Our Lady says, "You must realise that Satan exists. He destroys marriages creating division among priests and he is responsible for obsessions and murders. You must protect yourself against these things through fasting and prayer especially community prayer. Carry blessed objects with you put them in your home and restore the use of holy water." (Our Lady to the prayer group in the early years of the apparitions) We must know about the existence of the demons, though many people do not believe they exist, because we must fight against them and resist them. If you are on a battlefield, which we are, and you ignore the enemy, you are defeated before you even start. We must know about the existence of the demons so that we may fight against them and resist them. The best way to fight against them and to defeat them is to have Jesus' power within us which means through prayer and through fasting.

The Rosary is an incredible weapon against Satan, and

Mary tells us this so often in Medjugorje, because when we pray the Rosary, we place ourselves and our family under the mantle of Our Lady, and Satan has never been able to touch her. If you are under her mantle, you will be safe, but for that you must belong to her in a real way which means to live her messages, to live the Gospel, not only in words but in deeds.

Our Lady says, "Dear children, do not allow Satan to take control of your heart so that you become an image of him and not of me." (January 30, 1986) She also says, "Dear children, do not be afraid of Satan, that's not worth the trouble because with a humble prayer and an ardent love one can disarm him." (To the prayer group, toward the beginning of July 1985)

You do not need to be afraid of Satan if you are with Jesus and Mary. He is the one to be afraid. He is terrified even by a little child who prays. On the contrary, if you are not with Jesus, if you are not in the state of grace and if you want sin then please be afraid of Satan because you are in trouble. He has access to you and he will harm you. When I say be afraid of him, I mean may this fear lead you to confession and change your life. Do not remain in that fear.

The Angels and the Eucharist

Angels are divided into nine choirs: Angels, Archangels, Virtues, Powers, Principalities, Dominations, Thrones, Cherubim and Seraphim. Each order has a special role and position in heaven. There are special Angels for the churches and they watch over the churches. For example, if you go to a church and the Blessed Sacrament is there, sometimes it is alone because nobody comes to visit the Blessed Sacrament; Jesus is left alone. But just know that because there are billions of Angels, there are always a few Angels present by the Blessed Sacrament, and because Our Lady adores God in heaven, she is always adoring Jesus. So once again we have the invisible world that is so real. With your eyes you see only the tabernacle with nobody around but there are always several angels present.

When a Mass is celebrated, thousands of Angels congregate around the altar to celebrate Mass with the heavenly court. Not only the Angels but Archangels too—the whole heavenly Church. Our Lady herself is there at each Mass as well as the saints, and believe me among the saints you will find people from your own family. If your mother has died and is in heaven, she will be there near the altar.

In Medjugorje the Blessed Mother talks about the Eucharist, "If you knew dear children the graces and the gifts you receive during Mass you would go to Mass every day and you would prepare for it at least an hour beforehand." She also says, "Instead dear children when you are at Mass you are unaware."

She is right, we are unaware of what is really happening on the altar, but it is so beautiful when we start to see, with the eyes of faith and the eyes of the heart, what happens during Mass. This is why it is so important for us to go to church ahead of time to prepare our hearts for Mass. Not only to prepare to receive Jesus but also to put ourselves in the presence of God, in the presence of the Heavenly court that is going to celebrate from heaven this incredible mystery of the Eucharist with us and with the priests.

Pope John XXIII took great delight in the Angels and would call on them for important things, as well as day to day tasks. For example, when he had an important meeting with the Cardinals, with the Bishops and with VIPs he would ask his friends to send him their Guardian Angels during the meeting. When he had to meet someone, he would send ahead of him his Guardian Angel to prepare the heart of that person before he would meet him.

We can do that too! For example, say to your Guardian Angel, "My dear Angel, I thank you for your help, I am very happy about our friendship and the special grace of having you. I am grateful to God for you being by my side and being my best friend. I would like you to do a little favour for me, could you go to that town at that particular meeting and please make sure everything that happens there accords with the will of God?"

So, when you know you have to meet someone: your boss, your wife, your child, your teenager, your priest, your enemy, etc. ask your Guardian Angel to prepare the heart of that person in the right way. For example, if you are taken to court and you know that you are innocent, then you can send your Guardian Angel ahead of you to the judge and you can also send your Guardian Angel to the guy who is harming you and accusing you. Tell your Angel to calm this guy down and prevent him from harming you. For important appointments, just tell your Guardian Angels ahead of time and you will see the fruits for yourself.

When you are driving and you do not have a place to park your car your Guardian Angel is the one to find a space for you. They can also prevent accidents. I can testify that my Guardian Angel has saved me several times from death on the road.

If you are a mother or a father and you know that your child is in danger, or is in a bad relationship, or getting mixed up in drugs/alcohol then pray to their Guardian Angels and pray to your Guardian Angels to be there with them to protect them from bad influences and bad choices. How many times did St. Padre Pio say to his friends, "Send me your Guardian Angel," and he would himself send his Guardian Angel to his spiritual children or to people who were suffering in the hospital—he knew how powerful they are.

A friend of mine who lives in France has a very good relationship with his Guardian Angel. He entrusts him with the job of waking him up each morning at the exact time he needs to get up. One day he needed to wake up at 6 a.m. to get his flight home to France, but when he woke up, he noticed that it was 6:20. He questioned why his Guardian Angel did not wake him up at the time he asked him. However, when he reached the airport, he found that the flight was delayed by 20 minutes! He has not needed to set his alarm clock for years.

A name revealed

Sometimes in Scripture we see people talking with the Angels and asking them what their name is. Take the book of Tobit, the Archangel Raphael becomes a guide and companion for Tobias in his journey. He led Tobias to his cousin Sarah—he showed him the way and protected him along the journey. At the end we even see that he healed Tobit's sight (the father of Tobias). Now if you have not read this book yet, I encourage you to do so because it is fascinating. I love this book because it is very exciting and holy. At the end of the journey with Tobias the Archangel reveals his identity, he says, "I am Raphael, one of the seven Angels who stand in the glorious presence of the Lord, ready to serve him." (Tob 12:15)

It is possible to find out the name of our Guardian Angel—just ask him. Sometimes the Guardian Angels answer but it is not guaranteed. As for me, for years I called my Guardian Angel Raphael—I was a child when I started calling him that. But then one day I eventually asked him "Is this your real name? If it is not your real name, please reveal to me what your real name is." But he never did.

Sometimes we see people in the Scriptures ask the question "What is your name?" But often the Angels answer, "Why do you ask my name?" and then he disappears. (Judges 13:17-18) I do not know why some Angels give their name and some do not. Still, there is no harm asking the question, they may decide to reveal it to you. Some people say to me, "Why should I try? How can I try?" It's easy, just talk to him and say "My dear Angel, if you want me to call you more easily tell me your name, reveal to me your name," and the Angel has many ways to reveal his name to you. Most of the time it is through a dream.

Speaking of dreams, this is a story that happened to a member of my community, a very good lady. Unfortunately, she would never sing at Mass or during the liturgy because she felt she could not do it, she had an inhibition when it came to singing. She was very sad about it because we have beautiful songs and she would have liked to participate and so she often felt left out.

So, one day out of the blue I had a conversation with her about Angels and she said to me, "No, I have never asked the name of my Guardian Angel." So, I said "Do it!"

That day before she went to bed, she prayed to her Guardian Angel asking him to reveal his name to her. The next morning, I saw her all excited and she said, "Sister, sister, guess what? I had a dream last night and during my dream I saw a banner before my eyes and on that banner a word was written. But it's a shame because I don't understand what the word is, but the word was very clear and it was written 'shofar'."

I said "Oh my gosh!"

Knowing a little bit of Hebrew I knew that shofar is an instrument used by the Levites in Jerusalem as well as the singers and those in charge of the liturgy in the Temple of Jerusalem. It is exactly what she needed! Shofar is the horn of an animal; it is hollow inside and when you blow this horn it makes an incredible call. At the time of the Temple of

Jerusalem the shofar was used to tell the Jews when it was a time of prayer. The sound is very deep, it penetrates you in a very powerful way and from that sound everyone in Jerusalem would know when Shabbat or any big feast day was. You can find passages in the scriptures which speaks about the shofar, the instrument of praising God.

The name of our Guardian Angel can be an indication of our own vocation, and I explained this to my sister. She was astounded! Immediately she understood that it was a sign for her that she too should participate in the liturgy.

I told her, "You have this gift of music from your Guardian Angel and he will help you. Pray to him that he helps you sing."

The very next day she started singing with us! Her Angel helped to remove this inhibition she had about singing and it was not by chance that he was a shofar which meant that he was a musician before God.

When you think you have found the name of your Angel, if you understand the name then that's good, keep it. But if you do not understand the name, please do not use it. Do not call on a name that you don't understand. Why? Because demons also have names. The enemy is always trying to mimic what God does.

Let me explain, in some practices that are wrong, for example yoga, transcendental meditation, Ouija boards, divination and all kinds of wrong things that are actually called an abomination in the eyes of God (Deut 18:10-12), you can be given a word or a name. Sometimes you are given a mantra and you are supposed to use that word/phrase and repeat it constantly. You must also keep it secret; you are not supposed to tell anyone. Please never use any mantra, do not do it, it is dangerous.

I will tell you a story of a friend of mine who went to a university in North America. This particular university offered students a class on transcendental meditation, which is very bad. My friend and his wife decided to join the course. He was not warned against this practice and they spent nine weeks training to prepare to receive their mantra. At the end of the training there was a special ceremony in Sanskrit where the teacher whispered in each of the students' ear their mantra. They were told never to tell anyone the mantra but to constantly repeat it.

With transcendental meditation he would spend half an hour every morning and evening sitting in a certain position and repeating the mantra. My friend was not very prudent—he took the advice of this teacher and would constantly repeat this mantra to himself. During the course the teacher showed them studies showing that doing transcendental meditation would improve their IQ, would bring them more peace, etc. But what happened in my friend's life was that within a few months of him starting this practice with his wife, their marriage fell apart. They separated and almost divorced. It was a complete tragedy for the family. They had just had their first child and the mother was pregnant with another child. They suffered a lot—my friend became very anxious. He was distraught, very troubled and the more troubled he felt, the more he would repeat that mantra because it was supposed to help to bring him spiritual peace.

By the grace of God some good Christian friends helped him turn away from this practice. He reconciled with his wife and now they have a large beautiful Catholic family. Later he found a book that translated all the Sanskrit used in the transcendental meditation ceremony and he discovered that this mantra that he was given was actually the name of a demon! So, all that time he was meditating with his mantra he was actually calling on a demon.

When you do that, sooner or later they come, they do not need to be called twice! They are more than happy to come and harm you. So please never use a name that you do not know. It might be a good name but it is prudent to avoid it if you don't know the meaning. Do not run the risk to become infested. Most of the time I notice that the names of the Guardian Angels we receive are from a Semitic language, Hebrew for example, so if you do not understand the name you receive, go to someone who knows those languages and make sure the name has a holy meaning.

Just after the Feast of the Guardian Angels, which is on October 2nd, the visionary Marija Pavlovic received some homework from Our Lady. After her daily apparition the friend she was with noticed that she looked a little puzzled. Marija shared with her friend that when Our Lady appeared she said, "Today, I ask all of you present in the room," there were about five friends with her, "to make friends with your Guardian Angels and to seek their help and also I ask you to write a letter to your Guardian Angels and you will give it to me tomorrow." (Our Lady's message to the prayer group in the early years of the apparitions)

Her friends were a bit embarrassed at first because they had never done this and some of them had never even thought that they had a Guardian Angel. However, each of them complied and the next day they each handed the letters to Marija before the apparition so that they could be given to the Blessed Mother. When she appeared that day, Our Lady had five Angels by her side, so Marija assumed that these Angels were the Guardian Angels of the five people present. After they had written these letters and given them to Our Lady, they were very excited about the Angels and they tried their best to develop a relationship with their Angel.

They started speaking about their Guardian Angels and they noticed the parts of scripture that spoke about them.

They found out a lot about the Angels and they were very excited to finally make friends with their own Guardian Angel. They would ask them for favours and send them on missions here and there, they would use them, they would confide in them, they would seek their help and all sorts of adventures happened to them because of the Angels.

I guess what Our Lady said to them, she might say to you too, so I invite you to write a letter to your Guardian Angel and then place the letter under an icon or statue of Our Lady. She will be very happy. Afterwards you can keep the letter for a while and then you can burn it, it is your choice. But please make friends with them and ask your Guardian Angel to help you—it will change your life. Your Guardian Angel will manifest his love, care, and power to you. Your Guardian Angel is also the one who will take your prayers to God and who will bring the graces from God to you.

Many people today are suffering because they feel so lonely. However, they would not feel lonely if they could relate to a friend that is constantly by their side who is real, though invisible. Rest assured, if you make friends with your Angel, you will have many stories to tell your family and they in turn can start a relationship with their own Guardian Angel and it will spread.

You know, there is nothing sadder than a Guardian Angel sitting in the corner without a job. In this world where we have so much evil going on, so much violence, so much hatred, so much Satanism (it is increasing); we as Christians and Catholics are in charge of praying to our Guardian Angels and to all the Angels so that the peace in our world is restored.

We are the hands of God to promote that and to help the world with our Guardian Angels.

Now I encourage you to take a minute of silence to pray and speak to your Guardian Angel. Greet him, thank him, and ask him to manifest himself. Perhaps ask him to reveal his name to you. Take this minute to relate to him and see what happens.

> *"No evil shall befall you, no scourge come near your tent. For he will give his angels charge of you to guard you in all your ways. On their hands they will bear you up, lest you dash your foot against a stone."*

PSALM 91:10-12

Other books from the Author

- THE FORGOTTEN POWER
  OF FASTING
  Healing, Liberation, Joy . . .

- CHILDREN, HELP MY
  HEART TO TRIUMPH!

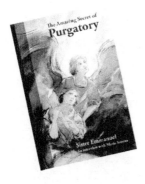

- THE AMAZING SECRET
  OF THE SOULS IN
  PURGATORY

- MARYAM OF BETHLEHEM,
  THE LITTLE ARAB

- THE BEAUTIFUL STORY
  OF MEDJUGORJE

- THE HIDDEN CHILD
  OF MEDJUGORJE

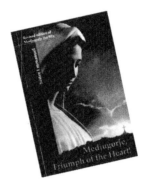

- PEACE WILL HAVE
  THE LAST WORD

- MEDJUGORJE, TRIUMPH
  OF THE HEART

- SCANDALOUS MERCY
  When God Goes Beyond
  the Boundaries

Printed in Great Britain
by Amazon